Investigating
Simple Organisms

Lisa Zamosky

Life Science Readers:
Investigating
Simple Organisms

Publishing Credits

Editorial Director
Dona Herweck Rice

Creative Director
Lee Aucoin

Associate Editor
Joshua BishopRoby

Illustration Manager
Timothy J. Bradley

Editor-in-Chief
Sharon Coan, M.S.Ed.

Publisher
Rachelle Cracchiolo, M.S.Ed.

Science Contributor
Sally Ride Science™

Science Consultants
Thomas R. Ciccone, B.S., M.A.Ed.,
    Chino Hills High School
Dr. Ronald Edwards,
    DePaul University

Teacher Created Materials
5301 Oceanus Drive
Huntington Beach, CA 92649-1030
http://www.tcmpub.com
ISBN 978-0-7439-0587-9
© 2008 Teacher Created Materials, Inc.
Reprinted 2011
Printed in China

Table of Contents

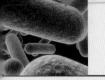

There are many different kinds of living things in the world. Scientists have ways of putting living things into groups. These groups are called **kingdoms**. For many centuries, scientists thought that there were only two kingdoms of living things. They were plants and animals.

A man named Anton van Leeuwenhoek (AN-tahn vahn LAY-vuhn-hook) was a scientist. He made fantastic **microscopes**. They made tiny things look bigger. Things that could not be seen with the human eye could now be seen. In 1673, Leeuwenhoek

Anton van Leeuwenhoek

looked at a drop of water under his microscope. What he saw shocked him. There were very small things swimming in the water. They were tiny, simple creatures that no one knew existed.

Leeuwenhoek called them animacules. Today we call them **microorganisms**. Another word for them is **microbe**. Scientists had to create four kingdoms for microorganisms: **bacteria**, archaea, protista, and **fungi**.

Leeuwenhoek's drawings of organisms ➡

Leeuwenhoek's Microscopes

Leeuwenhoek made some of the first microscopes. He built over 400 of them. Nine of them still exist today. Some people think he invented the microscope, but he didn't.

Leeuwenhoek studied the **organisms** inside people's mouths. At that time, most people did not clean their teeth. He saw creatures in the plaque he took from their mouths. He guessed that was what made their breath stink.

Sadly, the public did not believe Leeuwenhoek. He never taught anyone how to make his microscopes. He wouldn't share the ones he made. For almost 100 years, no one tried to repeat or add to his work.

one of Leeuwenhoek's microscopes

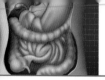

The Kernel Trick

There are many, many microorganisms on Earth. Scientists cannot count them all. They are all very different. The biggest difference is between prokaryotes (proh-KAR-ee-ohts) and eukaryotes (yoo-KAR-ee-ohts). *Prokaryote* means "before kernel." *Eukaryote* means "true kernel."

Both kinds of microbes have many **cell** parts inside them. In prokaryotes, the parts are mixed up together. Prokaryotes include bacteria and archaea. Eukaryotes include protists and fungi. Eukaryotes keep their cell parts in different places, like kernels on a corncob. They use **membranes** to keep their parts separated. Membranes are like walls inside the cell. Plants and animals have membranes, too.

Something called the *kernel trick* keeps things organized. It lets the cell get bigger and more complex. As a result, protists and fungi are much bigger than bacteria and archaea.

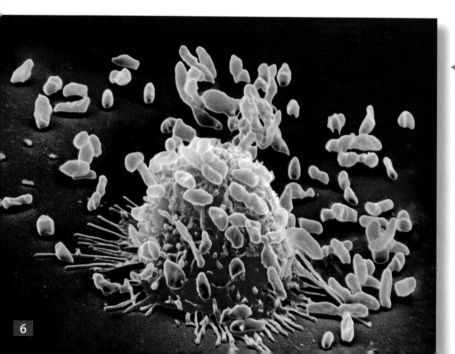

Prokaryotes are much smaller than eukaryotes. The white cells are bacteria. They are prokaryotes. The big red cell is a lymphocyte. It is a eukaryote.

bacteria (yellow) on the surface of the stomach

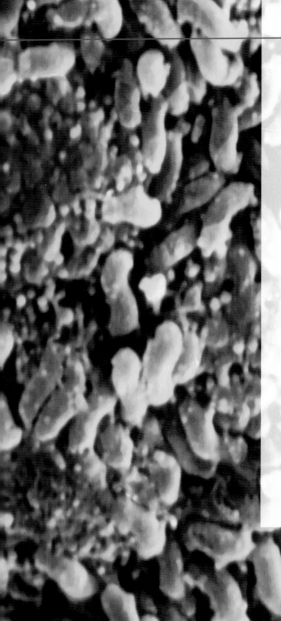

Home Sweet Home

Lots of bacteria make their home inside you. Billions of microbes are swimming in your digestive system. And they are crawling on your skin right now! Did you know that you have more microbes than your own cells in your body? At this moment, more bacteria live in your colon than the total number of people who have ever lived!

Ninety-five percent of all the cells in your body are microbes. They live mainly in your stomach and intestines. In fact, you have about two pounds of them in your gut. But they're not all bad. Some help you to break down your food.

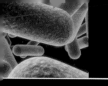

Bacteria and Archaea Kingdom

Scientists think that the first life forms were single cells. They were tiny prokaryotes. They had no cell membranes.

There are two kinds of prokaryotes. They are bacteria (bak-TEER-ee-uh) and archaea (AR-kee-uh). Both kinds can live in places that are very hot. They can also live in places that are freezing. There are thousands of **species** of prokaryotes in the world.

Bacteria come in one of three shapes. The first group is the largest. The bacteria in the group are shaped like rods. These rods often have hairs on them. The hairs are called **flagella** (fluh-JEL-uh). Flagella help the bacteria move from one place to another. Other bacteria are shaped like balls. They grow together in bunches, as grapes do. The third bacteria are spiral in shape. They look like corkscrews. They also have flagella that help them move from place to place.

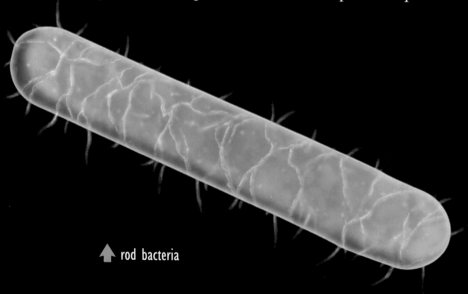

⬆ rod bacteria

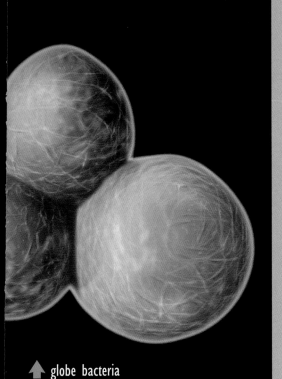

▲ globe bacteria

Big Bacteria

The largest bacterium ever found was the size of the period at the end of this sentence.

Why don't bacteria get big? They take food in and let waste out. They do it with **diffusion**. Diffusion makes particles move from areas where they are close together to where they are spread out. There is less food outside a cell than within it. So the food will move into the cell. As a cell gets bigger, nutrients get used up before they reach the center. If a bacterium gets too big, its insides starve!

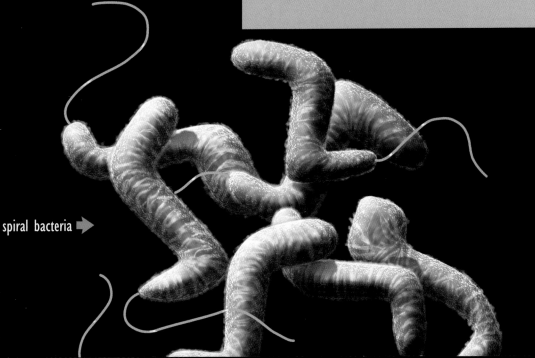

spiral bacteria ➡

Protista Kingdom

The living things in the Protista Kingdom are called protists. Protists are eukaryotes. They have cell membranes keeping their insides organized. They are much bigger than bacteria and archaea. They can also do some things that the prokaryotes can't.

Like bacteria and archaea, protists have only one cell. Some protists stick together. They form colonies. The individual cells still eat and **reproduce** themselves. They just work better if they are side by side.

Some protists behave like plants in some ways. They can make food from sunlight. This is called **photosynthesis** (foh-toh-SIN-thuh-sis). The protist uses air and water to make food. This also releases a little oxygen. Each protist only makes a little oxygen, but there are lots of them. If you add them up, they make a whole lot of oxygen. Together, these protists produce most of the oxygen we breathe!

These protists have formed ➡ colonies in ball shapes.

▲ The protists here are linked together in long strings. The strings wave back and forth in the water. This lets the colony capture more sunlight.

Now, That's Old!
The first protist probably existed 1.7 billion years ago.

plankton

Diatoms

Diatoms (DIE-uh-toms) are a type of protist. They are one of many microorganisms that float in the sea. These microorganisms are called **plankton**. Sea animals such as shrimp and crabs eat plankton. There are more than 5,000 kinds of diatoms in the world. They are a very important part of the food chain.

Diatoms have outer shells made of silicon (SIL-i-kon). That is the same thing that glass is made of. Diatoms come in many

Diatom

The bottom shell of each diatom is the smaller half. It splits and grows a new half. The newly formed whole is smaller than the original diatom. After many generations, the shells may become too small to contain the contents of the cell. When this happens, the diatom either dies or leaves its shell. If it leaves its shell, it becomes a **spore**.

Diatom Uses

Humans use the outer shells from diatoms. They make things that we use in our daily lives. The grit in toothpaste is often made of these shells. Sometimes shiny road paint is made from diatom shells as well.

different shapes. They are very beautiful to look at. Diatoms can be oval, round, or leaf-shaped. Some diatoms look like commas, and others like periods.

Diatoms reproduce by splitting their top and bottom shells. The contents of the cell divide between the two parts. Each part grows another half to become whole.

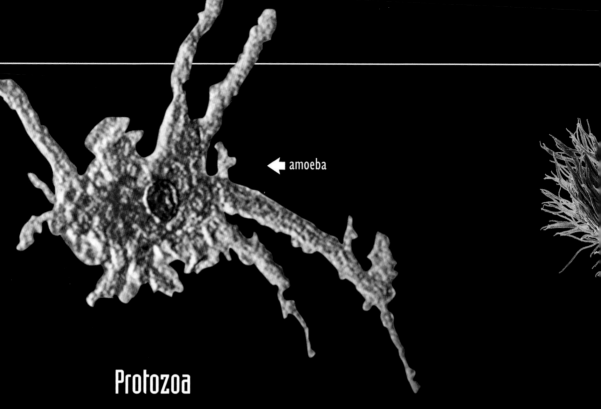

amoeba

Protozoa

Protozoa (pro-tuh-ZOH-uh) are protists that behave like little animals. They move around. They hunt other microbes for food. Mostly, they eat bacteria. There are more protozoa in the world than any other kind of organism.

Protozoa are single-celled organisms. They take in food through the tissue of their cells and through **pores**. Once protozoa **digest** their food, they give off nitrogen. This is a gas that other plants and animals need in order to live.

Protozoa fall into three categories. One group is the **amoebas** (uh-MEE-buhs). The second and largest group of protozoa is the **ciliates** (SIL-ee-its). The third group is the **flagellates** (FLAJ-uh-lits). The last group tends to be the smallest of all protozoa. They have long hairs that extend from their cells.

▲ ciliate

◄ flagellate

Lunar Quarantine

In July 1969, the *Apollo 11* astronauts landed on the moon. They spent 22 hours there. They took rock samples and made observations. Three days later, they returned to Earth.

When they arrived, they had to stay in **quarantine**. No one knew what "moon germs" or weird microbes they might have brought back. A new disease could make people ill! The astronauts stayed apart from other people for weeks. They were tested for strange infections. They didn't pick up any moon germs.

On August 10, they left quarantine. At last, they could hug their families.

Amoebas

Amoebas are very small organisms. They are about as big as the head of a pin. They are one of the simplest protozoa. Amoebas live in rivers and ponds. They can also be found on the leaves of plants that live in water.

The amoeba cell is made of a liquid. An outer membrane holds it together. For this reason, the shape of the amoeba changes all the time as it moves. The **nucleus** floats in the middle of the amoeba cell. The nucleus works as the amoeba's control center.

Amoebas take in water and oxygen through tiny holes in their cell membranes. They absorb food through their membranes because they do not have mouths.

An amoeba reproduces by dividing its nucleus. Then it separates the rest of the cell into two parts. If the cell were to split before the nucleus did, the half without the nucleus would die.

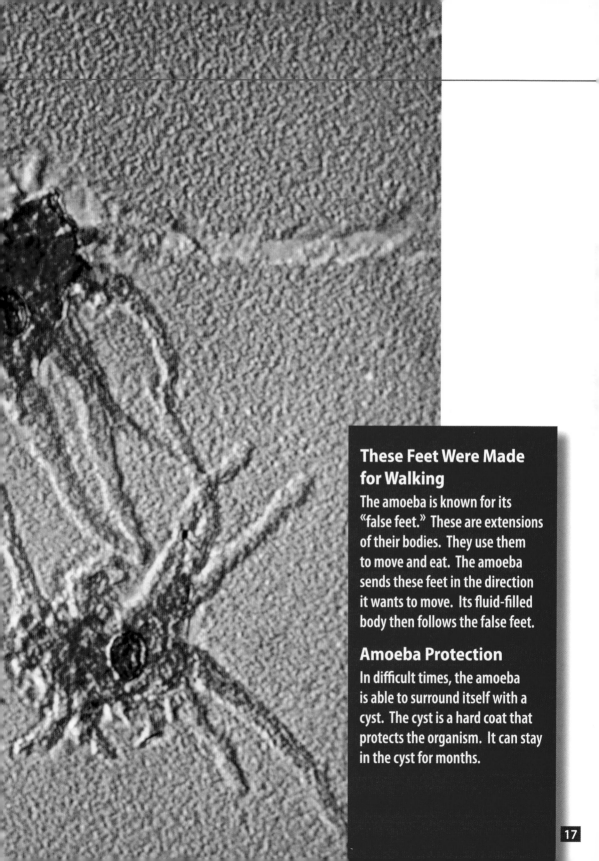

These Feet Were Made for Walking

The amoeba is known for its "false feet." These are extensions of their bodies. They use them to move and eat. The amoeba sends these feet in the direction it wants to move. Its fluid-filled body then follows the false feet.

Amoeba Protection

In difficult times, the amoeba is able to surround itself with a cyst. The cyst is a hard coat that protects the organism. It can stay in the cyst for months.

Ciliates

Ciliates are simple organisms. They move quickly. They move much faster, in fact, than the bacteria, protozoa, and amoebas already discussed. The reason for this is that ciliates have many **cilia** (SIL-ee-uh). These hairlike extensions look like eyelashes. They work like oars to move ciliates quickly through water.

There are more than 8,000 types of ciliates in the world. Scientists believe that even more ciliates exist than have been found. Ciliates live in every type of water you can imagine. They eat bacteria. So, they can most easily be found in places where natural things have started to rot. In fact, most ciliates are found in water with rotting plants and protists.

ciliate

Ciliate Protection

When the environment becomes harsh, ciliates are able to form a protective sac. They become smaller, and enclose themselves in the sac. When conditions improve, the sac opens up. The ciliate comes out to feed and reproduce.

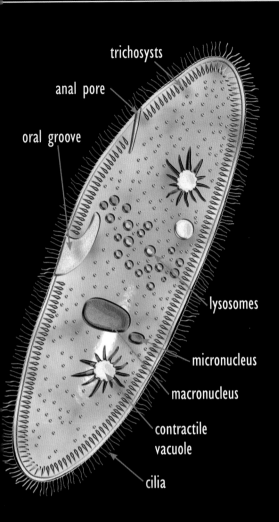

trichosysts
anal pore
oral groove
lysosomes
micronucleus
macronucleus
contractile vacuole
cilia

The most common ciliate is the **paramecium** (par-uh-MEE-see-uhm). You can see paramecia without the use of a microscope. They are big enough to see with your eyes. Looking into a body of water, they look like gray specks.

Paramecia have some interesting parts inside their cells. They have star-shaped **vacuoles** (VAK-yoo-ohls) at each end of their bodies. A vacuole is like a storage chamber. Paramecia live in freshwater that can enter into their bodies. If this happens, they could fill up with too much water and burst. The vacuoles pump out water and waste to keep this from happening.

Paramecia also have structures through their bodies called **trichocysts** (TRIKE-uh-sists). These structures look like rods. They give the protist its shape. Paramecia eat by pulling other organisms inside their cells. The trichocysts are used to hold the food in place while the paramecium eats it.

Paramecia reproduce by splitting in two. In time, those two paramecia will split into four. Then the four split into eight. It doesn't take long for one paramecium to turn into many separate organisms.

Complex Creatures?

These creatures are quite complex. Paramecia are able to move away from extreme temperatures and chemicals. If they eat something they don't like, they will know to stay away from it the next time.

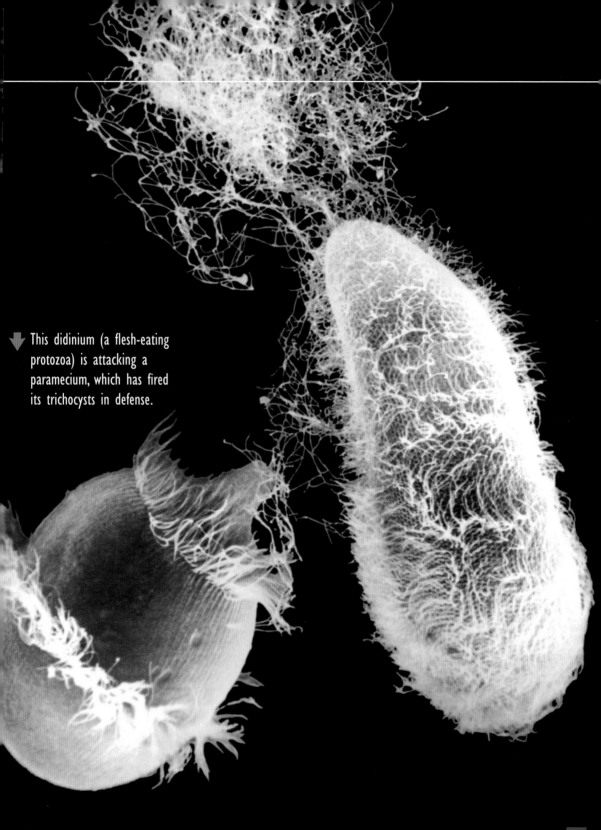

This didinium (a flesh-eating protozoa) is attacking a paramecium, which has fired its trichocysts in defense.

Fungi Kingdom

Scientists thought that fungi were organisms like plants. Then they found that fungi did some things the way animals do them. They cannot make their own food as plants do. In fact, they digest their food outside their bodies through their cell walls.

Fungi come in many different shapes and sizes. Some are single-celled organisms. **Yeast** is an example. One yeast is too small to see without a microscope. But lots of yeast can be seen on fruit or on leaves. It looks like a white powdery coating when it gathers as a large cluster.

Other kinds of fungi are multicelled organisms. They live in clusters. **Molds** are examples of this. Molds are simple **microscopic** organisms. They can be found almost everywhere. Molds form long threadlike strands of cells. The cells are called **hyphae** (HI-fuh). Hyphae create the fuzzy appearance of mold colonies.

bread mold showing hyphae cells

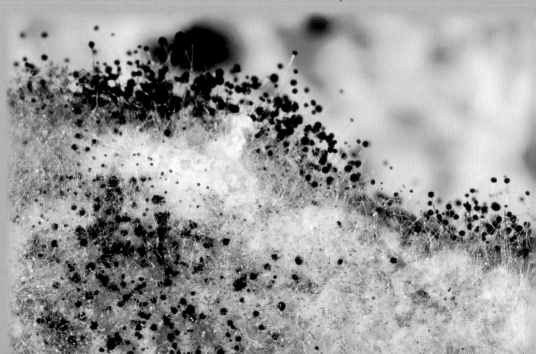

Important Discoveries

Louis Pasteur studied yeast. He found that there were two types. Some could be used to make food such as yogurt and wine. But other kinds would turn wine sour. He found that heating fluids like wine and milk killed the "bad" yeast. This process is called **pasteurization** (PAS-chuh-ri-ZAY-shun), after Pasteur. We still use it today.

In the late 1970s, a team of scientists found that bacteria could be used to make **insulin**. Insulin treats diabetes. For many years, insulin from animals had been used. But some people were allergic to it. Scientists found that they could feed the bacteria the human gene for insulin. Then, bacteria would make human insulin. Today there are bacteria farms that make insulin.

Rosalyn Sussman Yalow is among the most famous scientists who studied insulin to treat diabetes. In 1977, she won the Nobel Prize for her work.

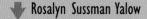
Louis Pasteur

Rosalyn Sussman Yalow

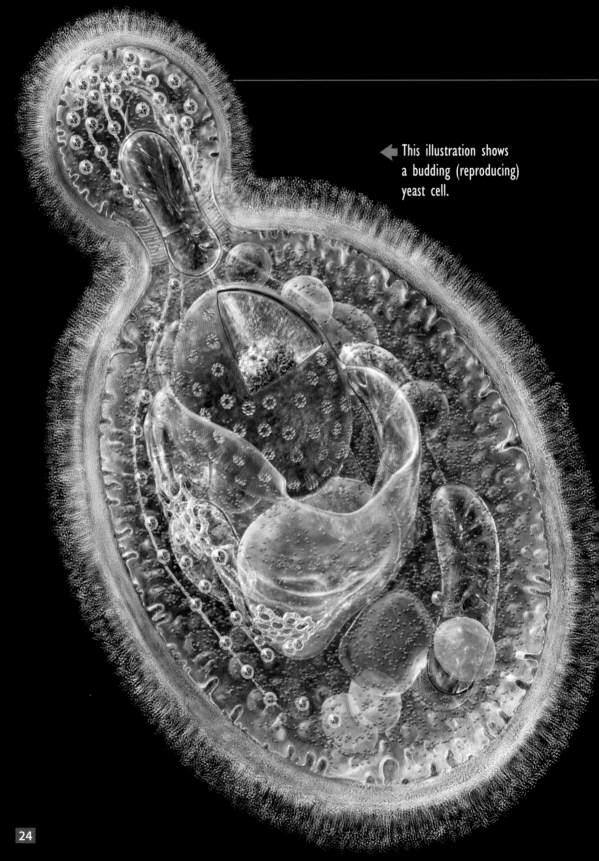

This illustration shows a budding (reproducing) yeast cell.

Fungi are able to reproduce in one of two ways. They can form spores that the wind and rain will carry. They also reproduce by growing their hyphae. Hyphae grow as new cells form at the tips. This makes for a longer chain of cells.

Fungi can be very useful. Several kinds of fungi are used to make **antibiotics**. Antibiotics fight bacterial infections. The fungi produce materials that fight bacteria in our bodies. We use another fungi, baker's yeast, a lot. We use it to make bread rise and to brew beer.

Some fungi are dangerous as well. They can cause diseases in plants, animals, and people. In fact, fungi ruin nearly half of all fruit and vegetable crops each year.

Baker's yeast makes dough rise.

Fungi, Fungi Everywhere!

Fungi can grow on things with very low moisture. They live in many places, including soil and your body. You can find mold in homes. You can find it on plants and animals. You can even find it in ponds and the ocean. A single teaspoon of topsoil contains about 120,000 fungi.

Mushrooms and toadstools are fungi.

Some of the organisms in this book have existed for billions of years. They are the oldest form of life on Earth. You cannot see the single-cell organisms with the naked eye. But they can be seen with microscopes. Microbes can be found in your drinking water. They can also be found in the air you breathe. They live in your stomach and on your skin. They keep humans and animals healthy. They also help to keep our environment clean.

Some of these organisms also have the ability to make us sick. We can thank early scientists for many of the tools we use today to fight disease caused by microorganisms. We are fortunate to know as much as we do about them and how they impact our lives.

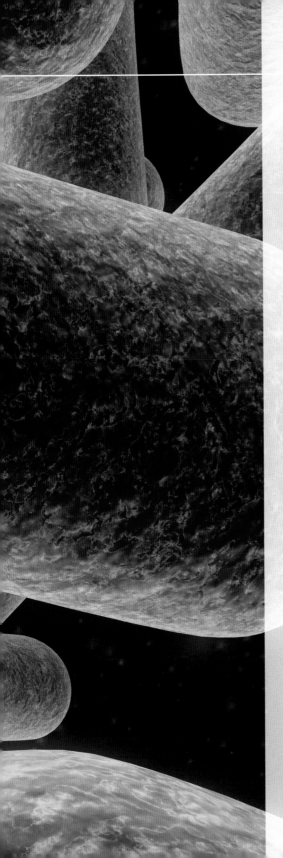

Wash Your Hands!

On every half-inch square of your skin, 100,000 microbes live. Most of them are harmless. But a few could make you ill. We call these germs. Those on your hands are most apt to enter your mouth or nose. Washing your hands for 15 seconds with soap and water will kill these germs.

Joseph Lister was the first surgeon who cleaned his hands and instruments before an operation. Before the mid-1900s, more people died from infection than from the operation! Surgeons seldom washed their hands. They reused bloody instruments! Today, all the tools are sterile. Everyone in the operating room scrubs for five minutes.

In this experiment, you and your partner will test how effective handwashing is in preventing the spread of germs.

Materials

- chart paper
- marking pens
- apron or smock
- washable paint

- timer or watch
- sink
- blindfold
- towels
- soap

Procedure

1   Create a comparison chart. Divide a sheet of paper into four sections with a marking pen. Draw an outline of a hand in each section. Shade in your idea of a hand that looks completely dirty, very dirty, dirty, and a little dirty. Label each section. Also, create two scoring charts. Label one Water. Label the other Water and Soap.

2   Choose one person to be the hand washer. Choose another to be the timekeeper.

3   Have the hand washer cover his or her hands with washable paint. Let the paint dry completely.

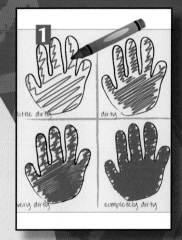

Go to the sink. Put a blindfold on the hand washer. Have the washer run his or her hands under water for one second. Have the time keeper dry the hand washer's hands by lightly touching the towel to the skin. (Do not rub off the paint.) Compare the washer's hands with the chart. On the Water scoring chart, record how clean the washer's hands are.

Have the washer wash for four more seconds with water. Again, lightly blot the washer's hands. Record how clean the hands are.

Have the washer wash for 15 seconds more with water. Blot and record the cleanliness.

Take the blindfold off. Allow the washer to completely clean his or her hands. Put the blindfold back on. Repeat steps 2 through 5, only this time have the washer use soap each time. Use the chart labeled Water and Soap.

Change roles. Repeat the activity until everyone has had a turn being the hand washer. Have the same person keep time.

Display your results. Create two graphs showing the average cleanliness score at each time interval. One graph will show the results when using water only. The other graph will show results when using water and soap.

Glossary

amoeba—a very small, simple organism consisting of only one cell

antibiotics—drugs that fight infections

bacteria—a type of very small organism that lives in air, water, earth, plants, and animals, often one which causes a disease

cell—the smallest structure of an organism that is alive

cilia—a microscopic hairlike structure that extends from the surface of a cell

ciliates—a class of protozoans marked by short hairs on all or parts of their bodies

diatom—a microscopic one-celled marine or freshwater protists having walls of silica

diffusion—the movement of molecules from an area in which they are highly concentrated to an area in which they are less concentrated

digest—to turn food into simpler chemicals that can be absorbed by the body

flagella—a long, threadlike appendage, especially a whiplike extension of certain cells or one-celled organisms, that helps the organism to move

flagellates—rods of hairlike structures that help bacteria and other microorganisms to move

fungi—molds, mildews, yeast, and mushrooms; a group of organisms lacking in chlorophyll and that eat nonliving matter

hyphae—the long, threadlike strands of cells

insulin—a hormone, produced by the pancreas, that is necessary for glucose to be able to enter the cells of the body and be used for energy

kingdom—one of the six categories into which natural organisms and objects are classified

membrane—a thin, flexible layer of tissue that keeps different parts of an organism separated from one another

microbe—a tiny life form, especially bacteria that cause disease

microorganism—a life form that is too small to see, especially bacteria

microscope—an instrument used to make very small objects appear larger

microscopic—extremely small object, especially so small that it can only be seen with a microscope

mold—a type of fungus that lives in a loose organization of cells

nucleus—the part of the cell that controls its behavior

organism—a living thing or system

paramecium—a freshwater ciliate protozoan, characteristically slipper-shaped and covered with cilia

pasteurization—heating a drink or other food in order to kill microorganisms that could cause disease, spoiling, or unwanted fermentation

photosynthesis—the process by which green plants make their food

plankton—small or microscopic organisms that float or drift in great numbers in fresh- or saltwater

pore—a tiny opening in the skin or membrane of an animal

protozoa—any of a large group of single-celled, usually microscopic organisms

quarantine—a period of time during which a person or animal that may have a disease is kept away from other people or animals so that the disease cannot spread

reproduce—to create offspring

species—a single distinct class of living creature with features that set it apart from others

spores—a single-celled reproductive body that grows into a new organism

trichocysts—rodlike structures in the body of paramecium

vacuoles—a hollow space in the cytoplasm of a cell

yeast—any of various single-celled fungi

Index

Sally Ride Science™ is an innovative content company dedicated to fueling young people's interests in science. Our publications and programs provide opportunities for students and teachers to explore the captivating world of science—from astrobiology to zoology. We bring science to life and show young people that science is creative, collaborative, fascinating, and fun.